ALEF	א
BET	ב
GIMMEL	ג
DALED	ד
HEH	ה
VAV	ו
ZAYIN	ז
CHET	ח
TET	ט
YOD	י
CHAF	כ
LAMED	ל
MEM	מ
NUN	נ
SAMECH	ס
AYIN	ע
PEH	פ
TSADI	צ
KOOF	ק
RESH	ר
SHIN	ש
TAF	ת

ISBN 0-915361-09-4

Library of Congress Catalog Card Number 84-09395
Copyright © E. Levin-Epstein-Modan, **1985**
POB 33316, Tel Aviv, Israel
Printed in Israel

A CHILD'S

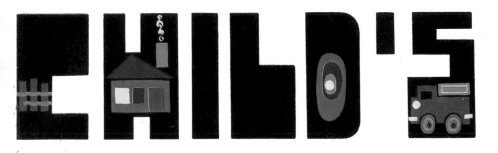

PICTURE

HEBREW

DICTIONARY

ILLUSTRATED BY ITA MESHI

ADAMA BOOKS NEW YORK

א

ALEF

אוֹטוֹ
o-to
CAR

BATH am-bat-ya אַמְבַּטְיָה

אֳנִיָּה
o-nee-ya
SHIP

אִמָּא
ee-ma
MOTHER

אַרְיֵה
ar-yeh
LION

אַבָּא
a-ba
FATHER

אוֹפַנַּיִם
o-fa-na-yim
BICYCLE

אִכָּר
ee-car
FARMER

אָמָן
o-man
ARTIST

אֹכֶל
o-chel
FOOD

אֲרֻבָּה
a-roo-ba
CHIMNEY

BET

בְּגָדִים
be-ga-deem
CLOTHES

בַּלָּשׁ
ba-lash
DETECTIVE

בֵּיצָה
bay-tsa
EGG

בַּיִת
ba-yit
HOUSE

בֻּבָּה
boo-ba
DOLL

בָּרָק
ba-rak
LIGHTNING

בַּרְבּוּר
bar-boor
SWAN

בָּנָנָה
ba-na-na
BANANA

בֶּרֶז
be-rez
FAUCET

STAGE ba-ma בָּמָה

בֵּית חֲרֹשֶׁת
bayt cha-ro-shet
FACTORY

GIMMEL

גֶּשֶׁם
ge-shem
RAIN

גָּבִיעַ
ga-vee-a
GOBLET

GARDEN gee-na גִּנָּה

גְּבִינָה
gvi-na
CHEESE

גָּמָל
ga-mal
CAMEL

F

גַּרְזֶן
gar-zen
AXE

FENCE ga-der גָּדֵר

גֶּזֶר
ge-zer
CARROT

גְּלִידָה
glee-da
ICE CREAM

גֶּשֶׁר
ge-sher
BRIDGE

DALED

דְּמָעוֹת
d'ma-ot
TEARS

דֶּרֶךְ
de-rech
ROAD

דְּבוֹרָה
d'vo-ra
BEE

דֻּבְדְּבָן
doov-de-van
CHERRY

דֹּב
dov
BEAR

דָּג
dag
FISH

דְּלִי
d'lee
PAIL

דֶּגֶל
de-gel
FLAG

דַּיָּג
da-yag
FISHERMAN

DOOR de-let דֶּלֶת

דַּוָּר
da-var
POSTMAN

HEH

har
הַר
MOUNTAIN

הוֹרִים
ho-reem
PARENTS

PALACE hay-chal הֵיכָל

הֲצָצָה
ha-tsa-tsa
PEEPING

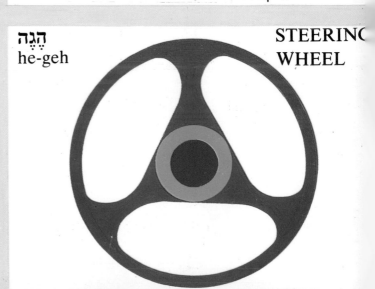

הֶגֶה
he-geh
STEERING
WHEEL

VAV

CURTAINS vee-lo-not וִילוֹנוֹת

וָאדִי
va-dee
DRY RIVER BED

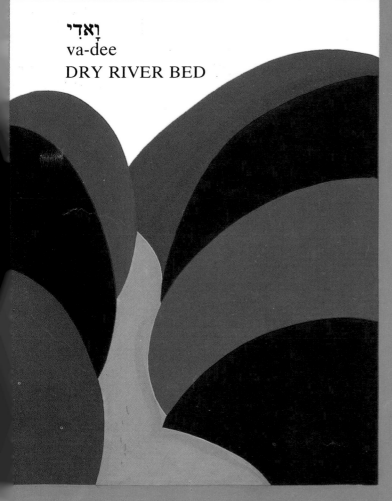

וָו
vav
HOOK

וֶרֶד
vered
ROSE

SUNRISE z'ree-cha זְרִיחָה

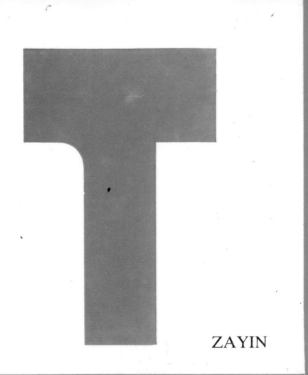

ZAYIN

זָקֵן
za-ken
OLD

INGER zam-mar זַמָּר

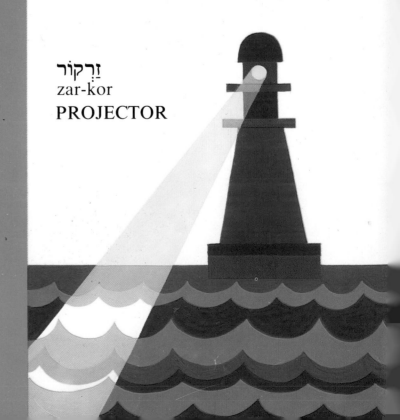

זַרְקוֹר
zar-kor
PROJECTOR

זוּג
zoog
PAIR

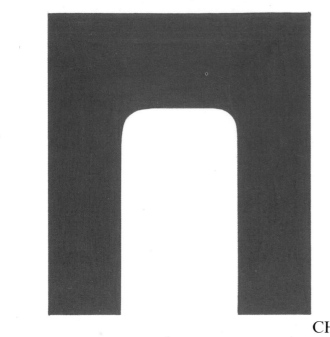

CHET

חִטָּה
chee-ta
WHEAT

חֲנֻכִּיָּה
cha-noo-kee-ya
CHANUKAH LAMP

STORE cha-noot חֲנוּת

חִיּוּךְ
chee-yooch
SMILE

חָתוּל
cha-tool
CAT

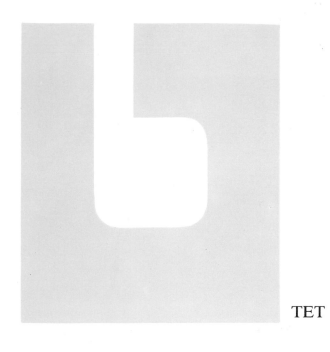

TET

טְבִיעָה
t'vee-a
DROWNING

טִיל
teel
MISSILE

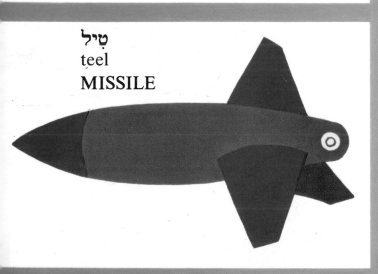

טַחֲנַת רוּחַ
ta-cha-nat roo-ach
WINDMILL

טִירָה
tee-ra
CITADEL

טִפָּה
tee-pa
DROP

טַבָּח
ta-bach
CHEF

טַיָּס
ta-yas
PILOT

טַבַּעַת
ta-ba-at
RING

טְרַקְטוֹר
trac-tor
TRACTOR

טַוָּס
ta-vas
PEACOCK

TELEPHONE te-le-fon טֶלֶפוֹן

YOD

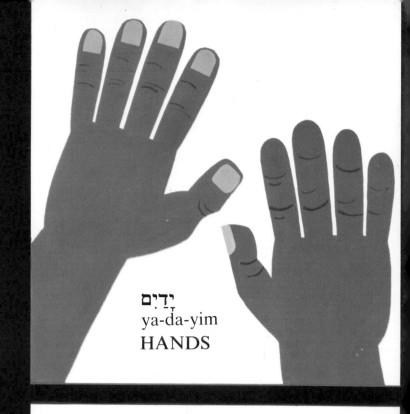

יָדַיִם
ya-da-yim
HANDS

יַעַר
ya-ar
FOREST

יוֹנָה
yo-na
DOVE

SCHOOL BAG yal-koot יַלְקוּט

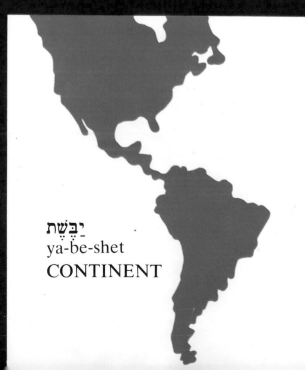

יַבֶּשֶׁת
ya-be-shet
CONTINENT

יָם
yam
SEA

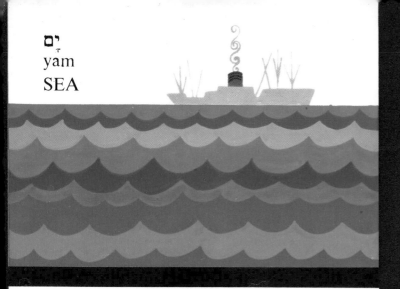

יֶלֶד
ye-led
BOY

יַלְדָּה
yal-da
GIRL

יָרֵחַ
ya-ray-ach
MOON

יָשֵׁן
ya-shen
SLEEPING

יַנְשׁוּף
yan-shoof
OWL

CHAF

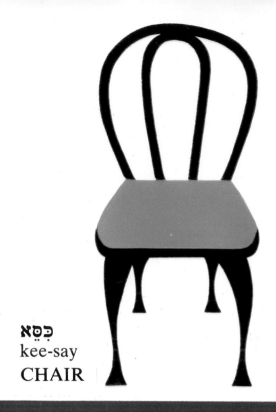

כִּסֵא
kee-say
CHAIR

כּוֹס
kos
GLASS

כּוֹבַע
ko-va
HAT

כַּדּוּר
ka-door
BALL

כַּפִּית
ka-peet
TEASPOON

LAMED

לֵיצָן
lay-tsan
CLOWN

לַיְלָה
lai-la
NIGHT

WHALE liv-ya-tan לִוְיָתָן

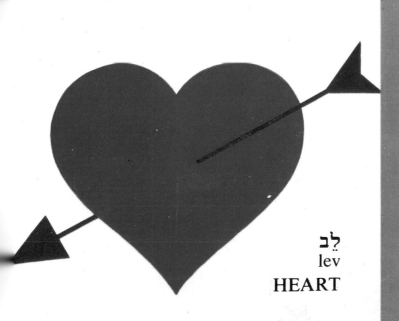

לֵב
lev
HEART

לוּחַ
loo-ach
CHALKBOARD

MEM

מִסְפָּרַיִם
mis-pa-ra-yim
SCISSORS

KITCHEN mit-bach מִטְבָּח

מַחֲבַת
mach-vat
FRYING PAN

COMB mas-rek מַסְרֵק

NUMBER mis-par מִסְפָּר

מִדְבָּר
mid-bar
DESERT

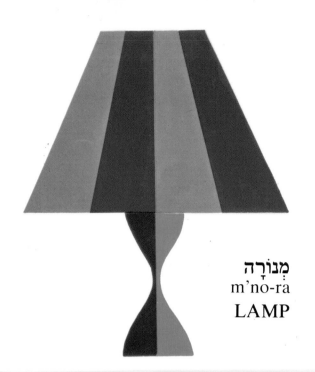

מְנוֹרָה
m'no-ra
LAMP

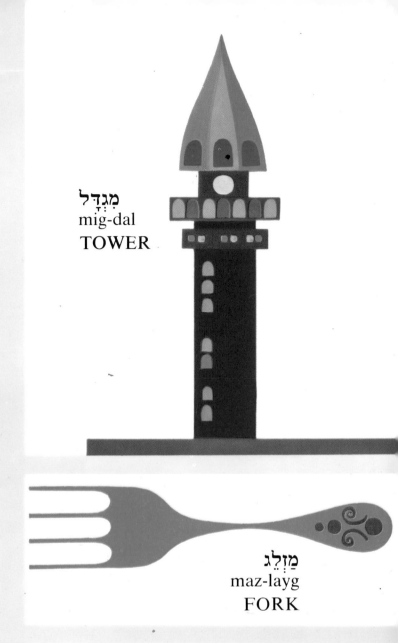

מִגְדָּל
mig-dal
TOWER

ENVELOPE ma-a-ta-fa מַעֲטָפָה

מַזְלֵג
maz-layg
FORK

מְעִיל
m'eel
COAT

מִטְרִיָּה
mit-ri-ya
UMBRELLA

NUN

נָהָר
na-har
RIVER

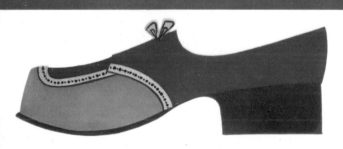

SHOE na-al יַעַל

נָחָשׁ
na-chash
SNAKE

נָמֵל
na-mal
PORT

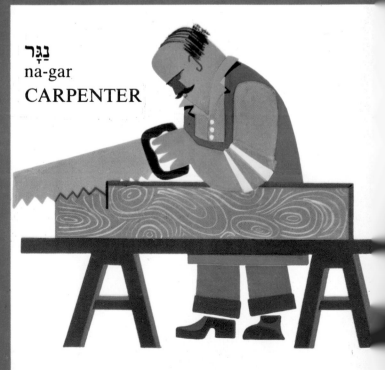

נַגָּר
na-gar
CARPENTER

נָשִׁים
na-sheem
WOMEN

נַדְנֵדָה
nad-ne-da
SEESAW

נוֹף
nof
PANORAMA

נַוָּד
na-vad
WANDERER

נֵר
ner
CANDLE

נְטִיעָה
ne-tee-ya
SAPLING

SAMECH

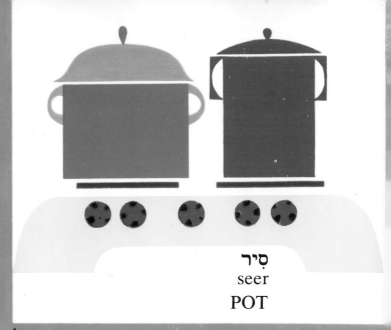

סִיר
seer
POT

סְיָד
sa-yad
WALL PAINTER

סוּס
soos
HORSE

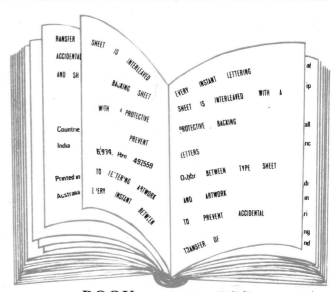

סַכִּין
sa-keen
KNIFE

BOOK   se-fer   סֵפֶר

סִירָה
see-ra
BOAT

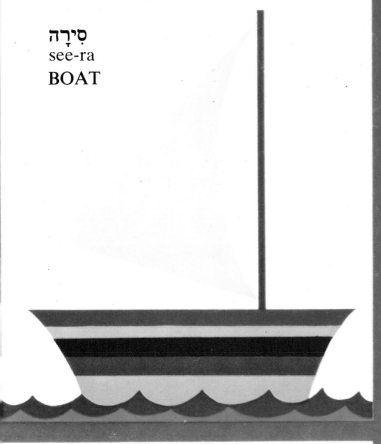

סַבְתָּא
sav-ta
GRANDMOTHER

סְבִיבוֹן
s'vi-von
SPINNING TOP

סִנָּר
see-nor
APRON

סַפְסָל
saf-sal
BENCH

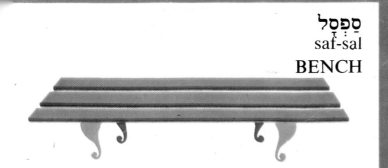

סַל
sal
BASKET

AYIN

CLOUDS a-na-neem עֲנָנִים

עָשָׁן
a-shan
SMOKE

עַגְבָנִיָּה
ag-va-nee-ya

TOMATO

עָלִים
a-leem
LEAVES

עֵינַיִם
ay-na-yim
EYES

עֵט
eyt
PEN

עֵץ
ayts
TREE

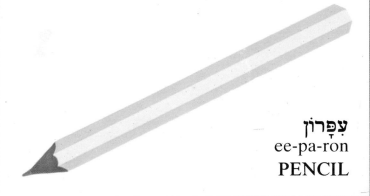

עִפָּרוֹן
ee-pa-ron
PENCIL

עוּגָה
oo-ga
CAKE

CITY eer עִיר

עֲגָלָה
a-ga-la
CARRIAGE

עִגּוּל
ee-gool
CIRCLE

PEH

פֵּרוֹת
pay-rot
FRUIT

ELEPHANT   peel   פִּיל

פַּטִּישׁ
pa-teesh
HAMMER

פַּרְפַּר
par-par
BUTTERFLY

פֶּה
peh
MOUTH

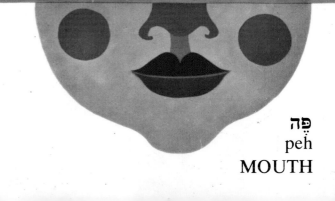

פָּנִים
pa-neem
FACE

פֶּרַח
pe-rach
FLOWER

פִּטְרִיָּה
pit-ree-ya
MUSHROOM

פַּעֲמוֹן
pa-a-mon
BELL

פְּסַנְתֵּר
psan-ter
PIANO

FLASHLIGHT pa-nas פָּנָס

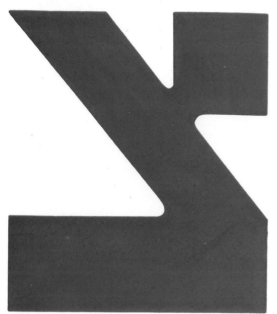

TSADI

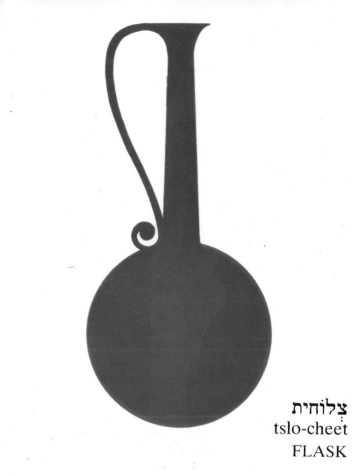

צְלוֹחִית
tslo-cheet
FLASK

צַעֲצוּעִים
tsa-a-tsu-im
TOYS

צִיּוּר
tsee-yor
DRAWING

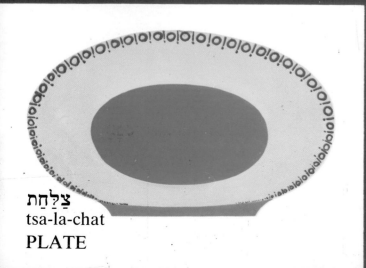

צַלַחַת
tsa-la-chat
PLATE

צָב
tsav
TURTLE

צָבָר
tsa-bar
CACTUS

צוֹלֶלֶת
tso-le-let
SUBMARINE

צִפּוֹר
tsee-por
BIRD

צֶמֶר
tse-mer
WOOL

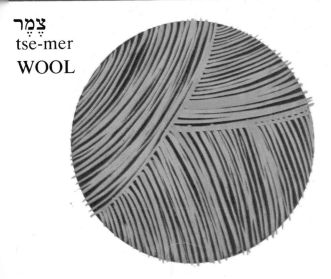

צֵל
tsel
SHADOW

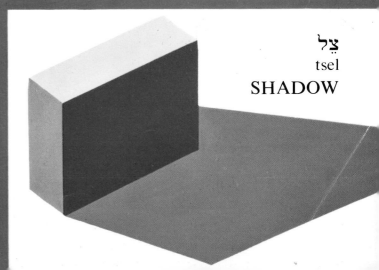

KOOF

קַבַּרְניט
ka-bar-neet
CAPTAIN

קוֹסֵם
ko-sem
MAGICIAN

קוֹף
kof
MONKEY

קֶשֶׁת
ke-shet
RAINBOW

KETTLE koom-koom קֻמְקוּם

קֻבִּיּוֹת
koo-bee-yot
CUBES

ANNOUNCER kar-yan קַרְיָן

קֵן
ken
NEST

קֻפְסָה
koof-sa
BOX

RESH

רְחוֹב
re-chov
STREET

רֶגֶל
re-gel
FOOT

רְהִיטִים
re-hee-teem
FURNITURE

רַכֶּבֶת
ra-ke-vet
TRAIN

רַמְזוֹר
ram-zor
TRAFFIC LIGHT

רְאִי
r'ee
MIRROR

רִיצָה
ree-tsa
RUNNING

רֹאשׁ
rosh
HEAD

רוֹפֵא
ro-feh
DOCTOR

רִבּוּ
ee-boo-ah
SQUARE

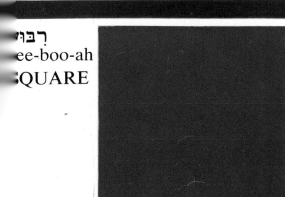

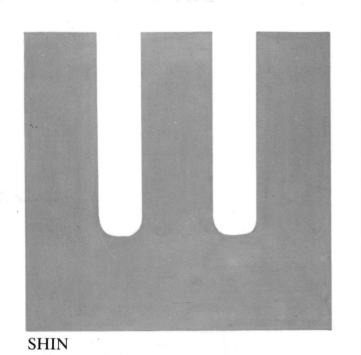

SHIN

שָׁמֵן
sha-men
FAT

שָׁמַיִם
sha-ma-yim
SKY

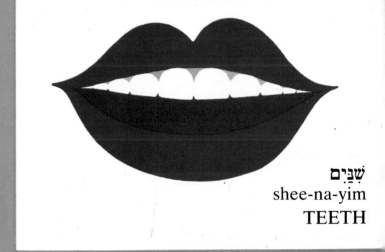

שִׁנַּיִם
shee-na-yim
TEETH

שְׁאֵלָה
sh'ay-la
QUESTION

שֶׁמֶשׁ
she-mesh
SUN

שְׂמִיכָה
s'mee-cha
BLANKET

שָׁעוֹן
sha-on
CLOCK

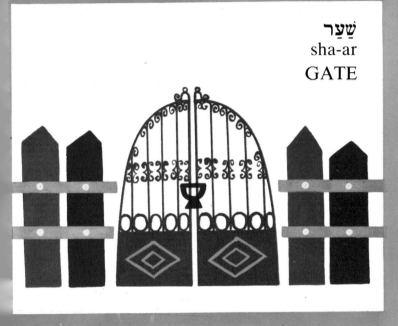

שַׁעַר
sha-ar
GATE

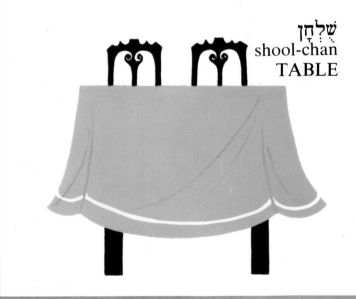

שֻׁלְחָן
shool-chan
TABLE

שְׂרֵפָה
s'ray-fa
FIRE

שָׁטִיחַ
sha-tee-ach
RUG

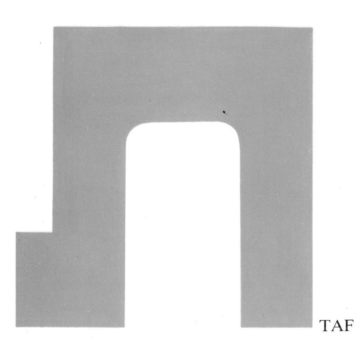

TAF

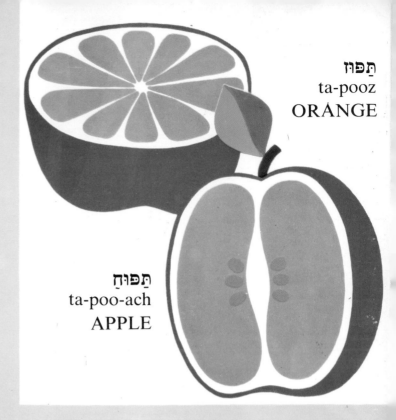

תַפּוּז
ta-pooz
ORANGE

תַפּוּחַ
ta-poo-ach
APPLE

תַכְשִׁיט
tach-sheet
JEWELRY

תֻּכִּי
too-kee
PARROT

תַנּוּר
ta-noor
STOVE

תְאוֹמוֹת
te-o-mot
TWINS

תֹּף
tof
DRUM

תָּמָר
ta-mar
DATE TREE

תִּינוֹק
tee-nok
INFANT

תִּזְמֹרֶת
tiz-mo-ret
ORCHESTRA

תַּרְנְגוֹל
tar-ne-gol
CHICKEN

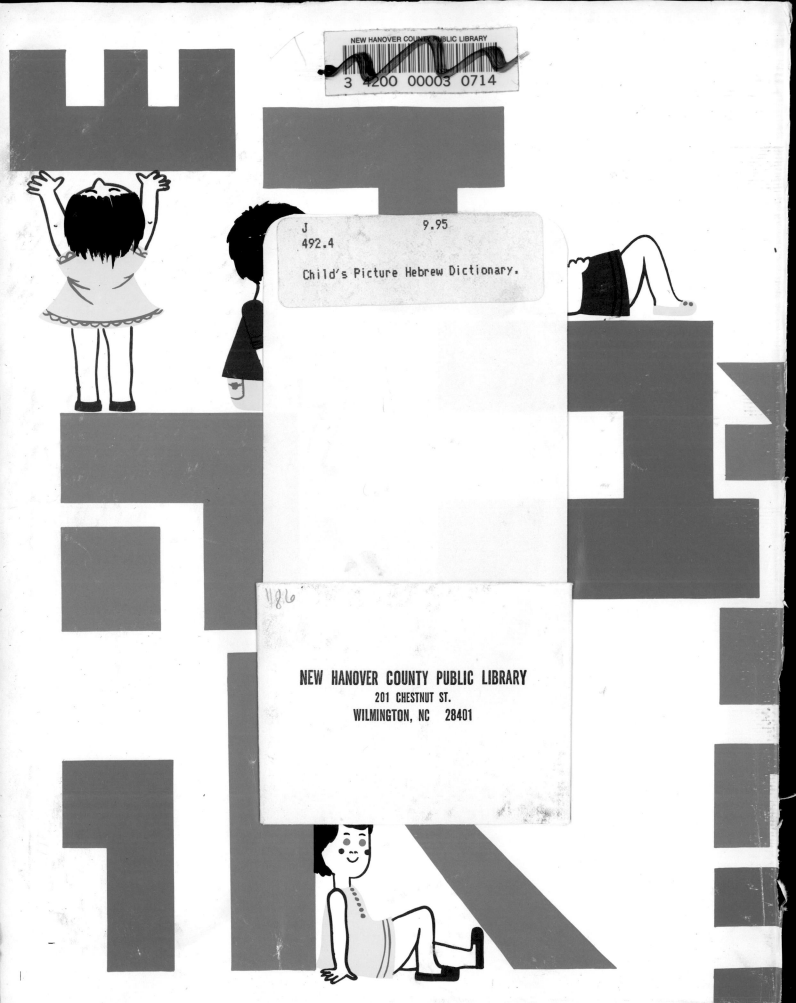